The
GREAT SALT LAKE
GUIDEBOOK

Dedication

*To the teachers who
prompted me to write this book,
and to the many devoted volunteers
with whom I have had
the pleasure of working.*

The
GREAT SALT LAKE
GUIDEBOOK

A Unique Educational Resource

Alan Millard

First Printing: July, 2000

International Standard Book Number:
0-88290-689-5

Horizon Publishers' Catalog and Order Number:
1265

Printed and distributed
in the United States of America by

& Distributors, Incorporated

Mailing Address:
P.O. Box 490
Bountiful, Utah 84011-0490

Street Address:
50 South 500 West
Bountiful, Utah 84010

Local Phone: (801) 295-9451
WATS (toll free): 1 (800) 453-0812
FAX: (801) 295-0196

E-mail: horizonp@burgoyne.com
Internet: http://www.horizonpublishers.com

Contents

5. The Great Salt Lake Today 43

Part 2
The Great Salt Lake Ecosystem

6. America's Inland Sea. 51

7. Plant and Animal Life Around the Lake 61

Part 3
Nature's Handiwork

Part 4
Material for Teachers

Introduction

Welcome to the Great Salt Lake! This educational guide will take you from ancient history to recent times, from lake to land exploration, and from bacteria to mammals. You will discover the ecological principles that apply here also apply to other aspects of nature and other locations. This guide provides information concerning many of the unique qualities of the Great Salt Lake, including its life forms and its weather patterns. It also will tell you about ancient Lake Bonneville and about the early exploration of the area.

Before you begin, try answering these questions:

- How was the lake formed?
- Was it always a saltwater lake?
- What do Hell's Canyon and the Great Salt Lake have in common?
- How important is the Great Salt Lake in providing a natural food source?
- What multi-million-dollar industries are dependent on the Great Salt Lake?
- How many species of birds rely on the Great Salt Lake for their existence?
- What types of ancient creatures existed here during the Lake Bonneville era?

These, and many other questions, are answered in this comprehensive guidebook.

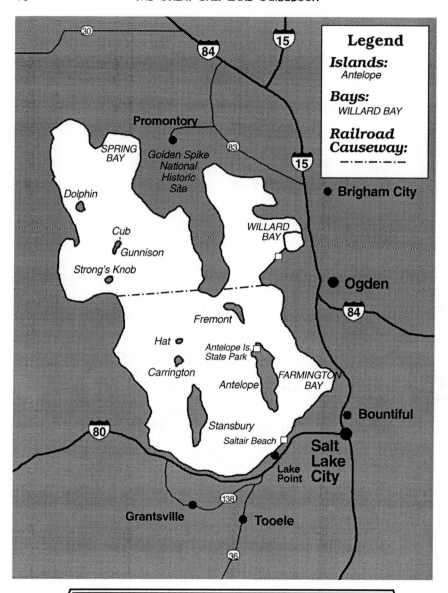

The Great Salt Lake
and Its Islands

Part 1

History

1

Lake Bonneville— Predecessor to the Great Salt Lake

An Ice Age Lake

The Great Salt Lake is the largest remnant of Lake Bonneville, a prehistoric freshwater lake that existed from 14,500 to 16,000 years ago. Lake Bonneville was 1,000 feet deep, 140 miles wide, and 285 miles long. It covered 20,000 square miles—an area that consisted of almost half of what is now Utah, plus parts of Southern Idaho and Eastern Nevada.

Two other remnants of Lake Bonneville also remain besides the Great Salt Lake—Utah Lake and Sevier Lake.

Lake Bonneville was formed by melting glaciers during the ice age and by volcanoes. A somewhat humid climate existed during the Lake Bonneville era.

Lake Bonneville Benchmarks

Terraces and plateaus on the mountainsides (which are referred to in modern times as *benchmarks*) are evidence of the changing shorelines of Lake Bonneville. Like rings on a bathtub, the different lake levels have left

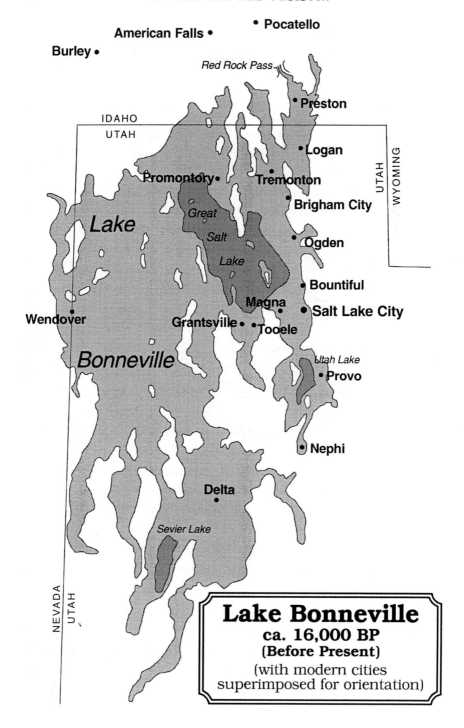

Lake Bonneville
ca. 16,000 BP
(Before Present)
(with modern cities superimposed for orientation)

their marks on the landscape. The most pronounced areas were ancient beaches.

The Bonneville, Provo and Stansbury benchmarks are prominent and easily distinguished along the base of the Wasatch Mountains. They can be seen in the Tooele Valley, on several of the islands in the lake, and from automobiles traveling the local highways.

Ancient bench marks can be seen along Interstate-80 in the Stansbury mountains south of the lake.

Lake Levels and Corresponding Bench Marks

The surrounding mountains bear tell-tale evidence of the varying depths of Lake Bonneville and, later, the Great Salt Lake, over the past 25,000 years. These are reflected in five benchmark levels: the *Great Salt Lake level*, the *Gilbert level*, the *Stansbury level*, the *Provo level*, and the *Bonneville level*, as shown on the following page:

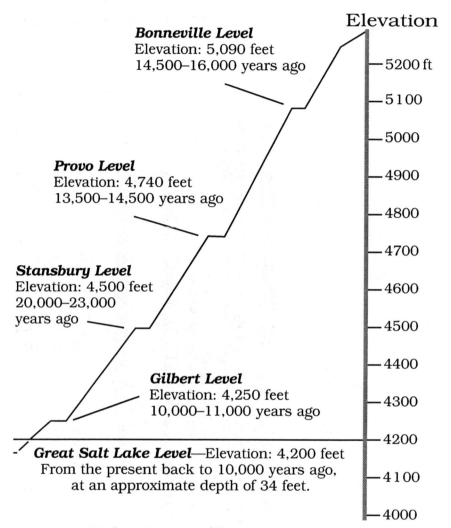

Elevation

Bonneville Level
Elevation: 5,090 feet
14,500–16,000 years ago

— 5200 ft

— 5100

— 5000

Provo Level
Elevation: 4,740 feet
13,500–14,500 years ago

— 4900

— 4800

— 4700

Stansbury Level
Elevation: 4,500 feet
20,000–23,000
years ago

— 4600

— 4500

— 4400

Gilbert Level
Elevation: 4,250 feet
10,000–11,000 years ago

— 4300

— 4200

Great Salt Lake Level—Elevation: 4,200 feet
From the present back to 10,000 years ago,
at an approximate depth of 34 feet.

— 4100

— 4000

Lake Bonneville Benchmarks

The Bonneville Flood

Water exiting from Lake Bonneville flowed north through Red Rock Pass at Zenda, Idaho, and exited into the Snake River drainage system. The water chiseled away the ground until reaching a softer rock material, which quickly gave way to the water's force. When

the natural dam broke, it created the Bonneville Flood, which carved out Hell's Canyon with its tremendous force. The lake level then dropped to what is referred to as the Provo level, with water still flowing out through Red Rock Pass at a much lower elevation (threshold).

If we follow the contour of the surrounding mountains and other land formations, we can see by the highest benchmark how large Lake Bonneville was before Hell's Canyon was formed. After reaching the Provo level, water gradually ceased to flow over Red Rock Pass, and a salt-water lake formed.

Lake Bonneville Sediment

In modern times, when drilling for water and minerals, some have found a thick layer of alluvium that was deposited on the bottom of Lake Bonneville as sediment. Lake Bonneville likely had much greater depth in its early years, but its depth decreased because of later sedimentation.

Underwater Volcanoes

Underwater volcanoes formed in the southern part of Lake Bonneville, many reaching above the lake's surface. These volcanic cones were formed between 12,000-24,000 years ago. Some can still be seen today approximately 15 miles southwest of Fillmore, Utah.

Volcanic cones have shot up through the Bonneville level. These are visible when traveling on Highway 257, south of Delta and West of Fillmore.

Fossils from the Lake Bonneville Era

Many fossil remains of fish and various animals, that existed during the glacial ages of Lake Bonneville, have been found. These include bones and skeletons of the woolly mammoth, the musk ox, the Monroc bear, the Bonneville cutthroat trout, ancient camels, buffaloes, bighorn sheep, and horses.

The Monroc bear was huge, about eight times larger than today's common black bear. Musk Oxen also roamed the shores of Lake Bonneville during the Pleistocene Age, about 12,000 to 75,000 years ago. The Bonneville cutthroat trout reached a large size. They could live in the waters then because Lake Bonneville was a freshwater lake.

*The musk ox roamed the shores of Lake Bonneville
in the Pleistocene era.*

2

Ancient Indian Cultures

Indians have lived in the Great Salt Lake region for many centuries. Evidence of their presence is prevalent on the islands and areas adjacent to the lake.

The first record of humans in Utah, dating 12,000 years ago, was discovered at Danger Cave, near Wendover, Utah. Humans living during this early period, 9,000 to 12,000 years ago, were referred to as the Paleo-Indian/Big Game Hunters. They were the forefathers of the Shoshoni, Ute, Goshute and Paiute Indians.

These nomadic groups hunted Pleistocene mammals such as Woolly Mammoths and ancient camels.

The opening to Danger Cave,
located north-east of Wendover.

*Pictoglyphs remain visible inside Jukebox Cave,
located approximately three miles north-east of Wendover.*

Well made ("fluted") projectile points were used to kill
these large mammals. These points have been found in
the Great Salt Lake area. Reliance on the killing of large
herbivores persisted from about 8,500 to 13,000 years
ago, between what is referred to as the Provo and
Gilbert lake-level periods.

Many other caves that harbored ancient humans
exist around the perimeter of the Great Salt Lake.

Buffalo were common in the Salt Lake valley until
about 1830-1833. Reliance on the buffalo by local Indians ceased at that time. Unlike Indians in other locations, they had alternate food sources to which they
could turn, such as migratory waterfowl, fish, deer,
antelope, rabbits and a variety of vegetation. They used
practically all parts of the cattail plant, not only for food
but for duck decoys, boats and clothing. Duck decoys
were found in a local cave which were found to be at
least 3,000 years old.

The settlement of the White Man on Indian soil has resulted in a variety of events and programs ranging from the tragic Bear River Massacre north of Preston Idaho (a wanton killing of many Shoshone[1]), to the founding of the Intermountain Indian School at Brigham City in 1950, which was designed to convert native Americans to the prevalent white culture. The latter was considered the Bureau of Indian Affairs' largest boarding school. It was part of a chain of programs that started with the DAWES Act of 1887, of which Alan Brinkley writes,

> Not only did they [the Bureau of Indian Affairs] try to move Indian families onto their own plots of land; they also took Indian children away from their families and sent them to boarding schools run by whites, where they believed the young people could be educated to abandon tribal ways.

---

1. All but exterminated by Col. Conner of the California Volunteers, seven out of 450 of this northwest band of Shoshone survived the massacre of January 29, 1863 (Shoshone-Bannock Tribal Museum, Fort Hall, Idaho).

Few Indians were prepared for this wrenching change from their traditional collective society to Western individualism. In any case, white administration of the program was so corrupt and inept, and Indian resistance so strong and enduring, that decades later, the government simply abandoned it.[2]

The school in Brigham City closed in 1984.

2. Alan Brinkley, *The Unfinished Nation—A Concise History of the American People*, 455.

3

Early Exploration and Pioneer Settlements

The Great Salt Lake has appeared on maps as early as 1710. One is the Lahoutan Map, named for explorer Baron Lahoutan, who based his chart on tales from Native American Indians about a large, salty lake. In 1776, Spanish priests, fathers Escalante and Francisco Dominguez, entered Utah Valley through Spanish Fork Canyon. Although they didn't see it for themselves, Ute Indians informed them of "a very large, salty lake" about fifty miles north. They took this more accurate report of the lake's existence to the outside world.

For many decades, the Great Salt Lake was depicted on maps of America as a half-legendary body of water. It was independently discovered in 1824-25 by two trappers, James (Jim) Bridger and Etienne Provost. Jim Bridger logically assumed the large body of salt water to be an arm of the Pacific Ocean. Not until 1843 was there any formal exploration of the lake. This was done by John Charles Fremont who, commissioned as a second lieutenant in the Topographical Corps, was sent to map the west and find (survey) the best route for immigrants to reach the west (primarily California).

Fremont's expedition sketched geographical features, conducted astronomical observations and explored the Great Salt Lake area. On his first expedition in 1843, Fremont and his crew almost perished in a rubber boat during a sudden storm. As record has it, they had to shoot sea-gulls (likely California Gulls), to appease their hunger.

Kit Carson, then with the Fremont exploration, carved a cross into a rock on Fremont Island, which is still visible today.

Kit Carson's cross, chalked in at the site for better visibility.
(Photo courtesy of the Stoddard Family)

Another survey, made by Howard Stansbury, followed in 1850. During this survey, Indians swam to Carrington Island and helped themselves to the red cloth used to cover the triangulation station.

As Fremont Island was named in honor of John Fremont, Stansbury Island was named after Howard Stansbury.

The Donner-Reed Immigrant Party

In August 1846, the Donner-Reed immigrant party, consisting of 87 members, 66 wagons and a herd of cattle, began to cross the Great Salt Lake Desert (today known as the "Salt Flats"), heading toward Pilot Peak (located on the west side of the desert in Nevada).

Seeking a short-cut to California they thought would save them 300 miles, the Donner-Reed party attempted the Hastings Cutoff. Lansford Hastings, author of *The Emigrant's Guide to Oregon and California,* was ahead of the Donner-Reed party with another immigrant group. Before descending into the Great Salt Lake Valley, James Reed, along with Charles Stanton and another man, rode ahead. They caught up with Hastings two days later at Black Rock, and persuaded him to go back and point out the best route to take. Due to hardships experienced by the Hasting's Party, he selected a different route, but his counsel this time proved to be more poor advice.

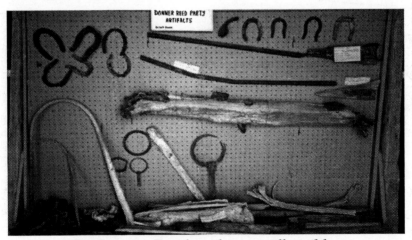

The Donner-Reed trail was still visible, including wagon ruts, until the area was flooded by the West Desert Pumping Project in 1987.

The group immediately began experiencing serious problems when they entered this extremely arid basin. Although many within the immigrant party wanted to recuperate in the Salt Lake Valley, time was already a limiting factor in their westward trek.

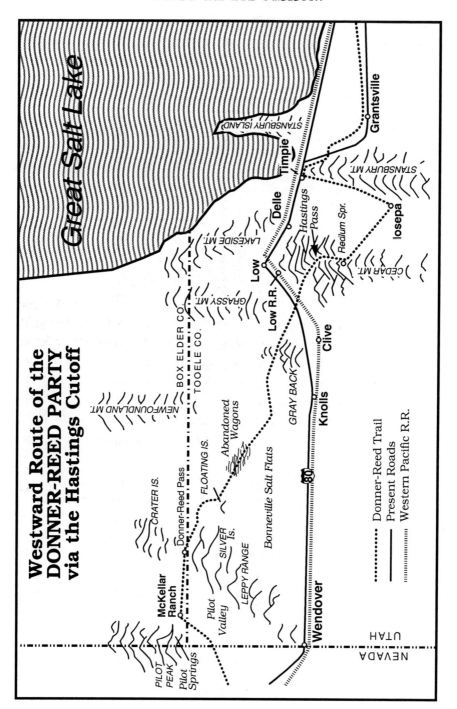

Westward Route of the
DONNER-REED PARTY
via the Hastings Cutoff

*Bits and pieces of the Donner-Reed party
are a silent testament of their tragic ordeal.*

West of the Great Salt Lake they encountered new problems. Their wagon wheels sank deep into the salt flats, they didn't take enough water, and they lost many oxen. Four of their wagons were abandoned ten miles after entering the salt flats. More time was lost. The mineral salt crystals cut the oxen's feet, and the salt ate into their wounds. As one source states:

> Their day and a half ordeal was marked by mired and abandoned wagons, runaway thirst-crazed animals and unbelievable human suffering. Because of these losses and delays, the party was caught by winter snows in the Sierras and only 47 persons reached their destination alive.[3]

Settlement by the Mormon Pioneers

The year after the Donner-Reed Party blazed their trail (1847), Mormon immigrants used the same route through Immigration Canyon to reach the Great Salt Lake Valley. Free from persecution in a place no one else wanted, the Mormon pioneers settled in the Salt Lake Valley.

---

3. Stokes, *The Great Salt Lake*, 28.

Brigham Young was disappointed at what he saw in the Salt Lake Valley compared to what he expected based on Fremont's journal. Nevertheless, despite the strong skepticism some of his party expressed, the valley proved to have fertile soil. Combined with a good local water supply, it produced bountiful food crops. The names of towns reflecting this agricultural value live on in the local community, names such as Bountiful and Farmington. However, due to continually expanding housing development, much of the most valuable farmland is now being destroyed.

The Great Salt Lake provided early pioneers an excellent source of salt. The salinity level of the lake was at 25% when they settled in the valley. By evaporating four gallons of lake water they obtained one gallon of salt. The salt was sold at a premium to other immigrants. Early Mormon settlers also did well raising food and livestock to sell and trade to other immigrants who were traveling westbound to California.

4

Development of the Great Salt Lake and Surrounding Area

W hole books could be written on the history and development of the Great Salt Lake and its environs. Though space limits what can be reviewed here, this chapter summarizes the highlights.

Fort Buenaventura

This was the first permanent Anglo settlement in the Great Basin. It marked the close of the exploration, trapping and trading era in the West. The fort was originally established in Ogden by Miles Goodyear in the early 1840s.

Salt Extraction Industry and Process

A permanent salt-extraction industry was established in the spring of 1850 after the immigration of the Mormon people. They first used kettles to boil off the water.

Major salt extraction began in the 1860s due to the silver-mining boom. Mineral salts were used to break down ore deposits, creating a high demand for the salt that could be extracted from the Great Salt Lake's

Lakeside factories, including this Akzo salt plant, process about 1.6 million tons of mineral and table salts each year.

water. This high demand for salt led to the search for improved methods of salt production and refining. About 1.6 million tons of mineral salts are removed yearly from the Great Salt Lake. Table salt (sodium chloride) is extracted in the largest amount, about 400,000 tons per year.

Magnesium, as well as other mineral salts, also is extracted from the water of Great Salt Lake. Being a light but strong metal, magnesium is used in airplane construction and for automobile wheels ("mags"). Magnesium is shipped by railroad boxcars.

Chlorine is extracted in the same process and shipped by railway tankers. Potash and calcium are extracted from the evaporation ponds too.

The Pony Express

Two-man stations along the Pony Express route were established for the care and shodding of the horses. This was an isolated and hazardous life. For receiving two riders per day, the stationkeepers were paid $50-$75 per month, the assistants, or "boys," about half that. They

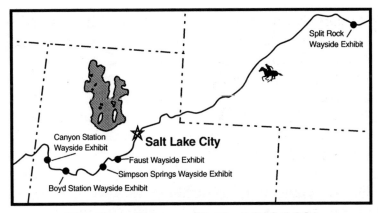

The Pony Express Route 1860-1861

lived on earthen floors, with boxes for furniture, and the roofs and windows were often ineffective. Pony Express riders were paid $120-$125 a month.

Boats

Boats on the Great Salt Lake included those used for exploration, transportation, freighting (ore, livestock, grain and supplies), and sight-seeing.

*Moored boats sleep in the same sunset
as seen on the cover of this book.*

Referred to as the Great Salt Lake Fleet, tug boats (such as the one named *Nevada*) and barges were used to transport fill material for the Lucin Cutoff. Fifty years earlier, Brigham Young, the Mormon leader, had a boat named *The Timely Gull* (launched in 1854) that was wrecked during a storm in 1860.

Other types of boats played a prominent role in the lake's history. The *City of Corrine* was a large paddleboat steamer. It was later renamed *General Garfield* in honor of U.S. President James Garfield who rode on the vessel before he became president. *Lady of the Lake* was another popular vessel. *Kate Conner, The Seagull,* and *The Mud Hen* were three other well-known vessels on the lake.

Resorts

Several popular resorts have existed on the shores of Great Salt Lake. These resorts offered dining, dancing, lodging, swimming, bath houses and boating excursions.

The original Saltair was a wonder to behold in its heyday.

Saltair, as seen in the 1990s.

In 1870 John W. Young (Brigham's third son) opened the first resort near Farmington. Due to the receding lake level, it was moved in 1894, to become what is present-day *Lagoon*.

Among the most popular resorts were *Black Rock, Garfield Beach, Saltair, Sunset Beach, Lake Park, Silver Sands Beach,* and *Lake Shore.* Their destinies were influenced mostly by nature in the form of fire, flooding, receding water, wind and wave action. The resorts were built on pilings over the water due to the lake's drastic fluctuations.

Saltair opened in 1893, but burned down in 1925. It was rebuilt, but the second version also burned down in 1971. All that remains of the original resort is an old concrete block building that was the train's electric generator station.

In 1981 a new Saltair resort was built, two-and-a-half miles west of the original site, and opened in 1983. The flood of 1983 to 1987 caused the lake level to rise, and the same year it opened, Saltair again met with a tragic set-back. It reopened in 1993 and is now the only resort left on the lake, representing a tribute to the original Saltair.

Sometimes considered one of the islands of Great Salt Lake during the lake's periodic high-water levels, Black Rock is acknowledged on the national historic register as part of the overland stage route and the early immigrant trail.

Black Rock is the grave site for the first two Anglos to be buried in the State of Utah. The two individuals were John Hargrave, a member of the Hastings party, and Luke Halloran, a member of the Donner-Reed party. Halloran was buried at the same location three weeks after Hargrave's burial. In 1933 the remains of two individuals, presumably Hargrave and Halloran, were unearthed by highway crews.

Black Rock is also known for the location of Black Rock Resort. It was a popular railroad stop for tourists.

Railroad

The *Lucin Cut-off* is a solid rock fill providing a railroad short-cut across the middle of Great Salt Lake. It spans the lake from west of Ogden to Lakeside. The cut-off was originally built by the railroad in 1903. Due to instability, it became necessary to build a wooden trestle for the last 12 miles of the causeway. About 38,000 wooden pilings had to be driven 120 feet into the ground. Although the water was only 20 to 35 feet deep, the pilings had to be 120 feet deep to ensure a firm platform. Some had to be placed end to end (240 feet deep) before they were secure enough to hold the trestle.

The original Lucin Cut-off railroad trestle.

Between 1955 and 1959, the wooden trestle was replaced with solid rock fill forming the present-day railroad causeway. Its construction was completed in 1959 by the Southern Pacific Railroad. Little Valley, the construction camp, was located about two miles north of Promontory Point. It was near the site that was blasted in July 1957 to obtain the needed fill.

The 1955-59 replacement project cost more than $50 million. This man-made barrier now divides the Great Salt Lake into a northern arm and a southern arm. In 1984, after a very wet cycle, so much water entered the southern arm of the lake that the railroad causeway unintentionally became a dam. Something had to be done to allow the water through, so a 300-ft. opening was blasted through the causeway, allowing excess southern lake water to enter the northern arm.

World War II Military Involvement

The Bonneville Salt Flats and Wendover area are known for their second world war military history. Slightly south-east of Wendover, Utah, bordering the Bonneville Salt Flats, is the Wendover Field military facility. During World War II, 20,000 military personnel were stationed there.

This is where the atomic bomb was assembled which was dropped on Japan, ending World War II. It is also the original home of the *Enola Gay*, the plane that dropped the bomb. The Enola Gay Hangar is a large, prominent structure in the southeastern out-skirts of Wendover that can be seen from several miles away, and has recently been restored.

What is now Danger Cave State Park and adjacent areas once included a bombing range through which a jeep robot was sent as a target.

The old military dance floor can still be seen
in Jukebox Cave today.
(The piles of dirt are from looters sifting for artifacts.

*The Enola Gay Hangar
is located south-east of Wendover, Utah.*

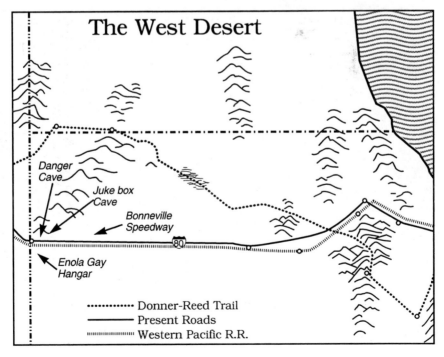

Jukebox Cave, also located in Danger Cave State Park, was named as a result of the military presence in the area during the war. A dance floor was built in the cave and a jukebox provided dance music for military personnel.

The Bonneville Salt Flats

The *Bonneville Raceway* is located within the Bonneville Salt Flats, northeast of Wendover, Utah, where the highest land speed record of 622 mph was set in 1970. The photo below was taken during "Speed Week '95."

The West Desert Pumping Project

Something had to be done about the flooding problem during the mid 1980's. The need resulted in the *West Desert Pumping Project.* In 1987, the Newfoundland

Great Salt Lake, Bonneville Salt Flats, and elements of the state's two flood-control programs: the causeway breach (1984) and the West Desert Pumping Project (1987).

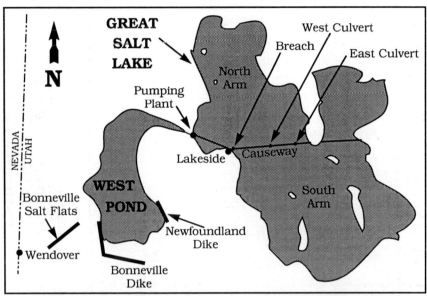

The West Desert pumping plant, on the west side of the Lucin cut-off. Water was pumped from the north arm of the lake through a 4.1-mile-long canal to the 320,000-acre West Pond.

(Photo courtesy of Ron Ollis, Public Affairs Officer, Department of Natural Resources, Division of Water Resources. Used by Permission)

Evaporation Basin, a 320,000-acre evaporation pond
northeast of Wendover was created by massive pumping
from the Great Salt Lake. The pumps were located on
the west shore adjacent to the Southern Pacific Railroad
causeway. However, within two years the basin was full,
and water began returning to the main lake. There was
no place left into which the water could be pumped. (The
increased lake surface area resulted in more evaporation, adding to the "lake effect," referred to later in this
book.) Fortunately, the excess water trend ceased at this
time. The pumping project cost $60 million.

Pilot Peak, at the west end of the Salt Flats.
This was considered "the light at the end of the tunnel"
for immigrants crossing the Great Salt Lake desert.

5

The Great Salt Lake Today

Recreation and Points of Interest

The sturdy **Saltair** pavilion that was flooded in 1983 still stands. It has been dried out and renewed, and is open for entertainment again. The only remnant of the historical resorts, it sports a snack bar, two gift shops, a stationary paddle wheel boat, and a place for dances and concerts.

Two Utah state park facilities exist on Great Salt Lake. These are the **Great Salt Lake State Marina** (formerly Great Salt Lake State Park) and **Antelope Island State Park.** The Great Salt Lake State Marina has a gift shop and borders Interstate 80, approximately 17 miles west of Salt Lake City. A cruise liner service, **Salt Island Adventures,** operates out of the Great Salt Lake Marina. (See tours for additional info.)

Antelope Island State Park encompasses all of Antelope Island, with most of its development (park facilities, including a boat harbor) located on the northern end.

The Buffalo Point snackbar and giftshop are open daily during the summer season and when fair weather conditions exist. Call 776-6734 for more information. The Antelope Island visitor center and giftshop is open seven days a week. Summer hours: 10am–5pm. Winter

Sunsets, such as this one over Stansbury Island,
attract and inspire artists and photographers.

hours: 10am–5pm weekends and 10am–4pm week-days. Call 725-9263 for more information.

Both park facilities have a marina with emergency communication base stations and emergency rescue personnel available. Channel 16 is the U.S. Coast Guard's emergency communications channel. Due to the sudden and severe storms that can develop on the lake, it is important to establish radio communications while boating on Great Salt Lake. Emergency rescue personnel can be called for help if needed.

Although **Willard Bay State Park** borders the lake to the northeast, Willard Bay Reservoir is a freshwater body. It has no boating access to the rest of the Great Salt Lake, and is separated from the salt water by dikes.

Willard Bay Reservoir rests atop the Great Salt Lake flood plain. Its 9,900 acres of fresh water provide boat-ing, waterskiing and year-round fishing for crappie, walleye, wiper and catfish. Camping is also popular at the park. Two state-owned facilities are available to

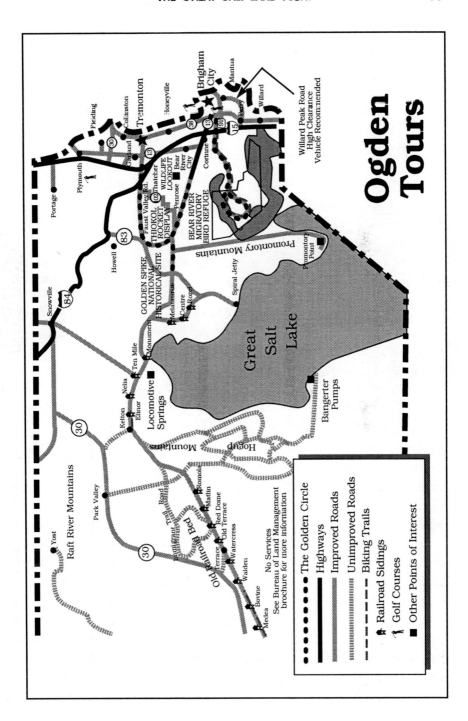

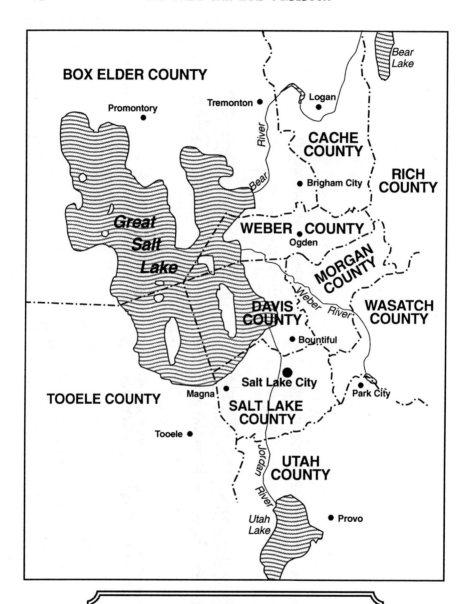

BOX ELDER COUNTY

Promontory

Tremonton

Logan

River

CACHE COUNTY

RICH COUNTY

Bear

Brigham City

Great Salt Lake

WEBER COUNTY

Ogden

MORGAN COUNTY

Weber River

DAVIS COUNTY

WASATCH COUNTY

Bountiful

Salt Lake City

Park City

TOOELE COUNTY

Magna

SALT LAKE COUNTY

Tooele

Jordan River

UTAH COUNTY

Utah Lake

Provo

Bear Lake

Counties Surrounding the Great Salt Lake

recreationists. The **North Marina** park has 64 camp-sites, modern rest rooms, hot showers, a sewage disposal station, seasonal/transient boat slip rentals and sandy beaches. The **South Marina** is open April through October and provides boat launching and modern rest rooms.

Fort Buenaventura has been reconstructed on a 32-acre tract of land in Ogden, 35 miles north of Salt Lake City. This state park includes stockade and cabin replicas on the original site, a visitor center, group camping and day-use area, picnic tables, canoe rentals and modern rest rooms.

The **Ogden Nature Center** is located at 966 West 12th Street, just minutes from downtown Ogden. The facility is open to the public Monday through Saturday, 10:00 a.m. to 4:00 p.m., Ph. 621-7595.

The **Ogden Union Station,** located at 2501 Wall Avenue, has two giftshops, a restaurant, a rocks and gems exhibit room, a railroad museum, and the **Browning Arms Museum** on the main floor. Ph. 393-9882.

The Salt Lake City **Rio Grande** building, located at 270 South Rio Grande (500 West), offers a restaurant, museum, giftshop and exhibits on the first floor. State History is located on the second floor, Ph. 533-3500 and 364-3302 (Cafe).

The **Tooele Railroad Museum** is located in downtown Tooele on Broadway and Vine streets. Open Tuesdays through Saturdays, 10am to 4pm, Memorial Day through Labor Day. Call 882-2836 for more information.

The **Donner-Reed Museum** is located in downtown Grantsville on the corner of Cooley and Clark streets. Call Ruth Matthews for tours at 884-3348.

The **Syracuse giftshop**/bed and breakfast is located on the north side of main street (Antelope Drive) in Syracuse. Phone 775-9114.

The **Museum of Natural History** is located at the University of Utah, President's Circle. Ph. 581-4303.

The **Layton Heritage** Museum is located at 403 Wasatch Drive at the city park just northwest of the high school. Call 546-8579.

Part 2

The Great Salt Lake Ecosystem

6

America's Inland Sea

With saltwater, brine shrimp and sea gulls, the Great Salt Lake is America's inland sea, the most extensive lake of its kind in the Western hemisphere. It is a land-locked body of water, so unique that it forms its own weather patterns.

Great Salt Lake ranks fourth in size among the major saltwater lakes of the world. However, it is second in size if we consider that the two largest saltwater lakes are actually classified as seas. The following chart shows their relative areas and salinity:

Comparative Sizes of Saltwater Lakes

Water body	Salinity (parts per thousand)	Area (square miles)
Caspian Sea (Russia, Iran)	11	170,000
Aral Sea (Russia)	10	25,000
Lake Balkhash (Russia)	2.8	7,115
Great Salt Lake (Utah)	*140	1,700
Salton Sea (California)	44	380
Dead Sea (Israel)	220	390
Mono Lake (California)	78	71.7

*Measurement for *Gilbert Bay*, 1995.

Salt Content

With the exception of the *Dead Sea* in Palestine, nothing quite like the Great Salt Lake exists. This large body of shallow, salty water has an average salt content of 25 per cent. that is eight times saltier than the ocean. In comparison, the *Dead Sea* has a 27 per cent saline content. The ocean is only 3 per cent.

The lake's salinity changes during dry and wet cycles. The highest recorded salinity is 27 per cent and the lowest is 5 per cent. A salt concentration content of 27.3 per cent is the highest percentage possible. When this level is reached, the mineral salts begin to crystallize (referred to as the saturation point). A small amount of mineral salt is present in the fresh water that flows into Great Salt Lake. The mineral salts deposited by incoming rivers have no escape. When the water evaporates, it leaves the salt behind. The more salt deposited by the freshwater, the more concentrated the lake becomes.

A Variable Coastline

Within the past century, the lake's size has varied from about 2,400 square miles to 700 square miles. Great Salt Lake varies in both width and length, being approximately 90 miles in length from north to south and 40 miles wide from east to west. Since Great Salt Lake exists at the bottom of the ancient Lake Bonneville, it expands over a flat, plate-like area and is very shallow. A rise in water level of only a few feet can extend the lake's shoreline by many miles.

A Shallow Lake

At an elevation of 4,200 feet, the lake reaches a maximum depth of about 34 feet, with an average depth of 13 feet. The depth varies from year to year, especially during multi-year wet/dry cycles.

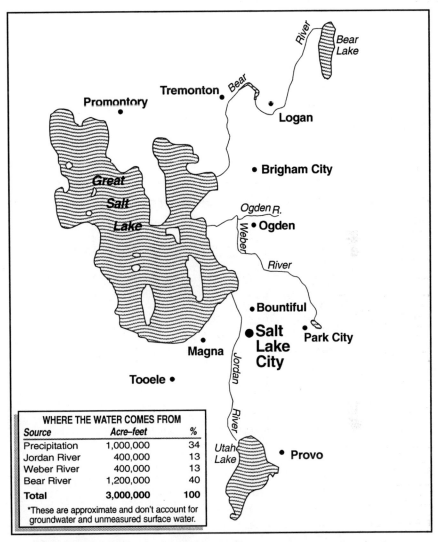

WHERE THE WATER COMES FROM		
Source	*Acre–feet*	*%*
Precipitation	1,000,000	34
Jordan River	400,000	13
Weber River	400,000	13
Bear River	1,200,000	40
Total	**3,000,000**	**100**

*These are approximate and don't account for groundwater and unmeasured surface water.

Great Salt Lake is fed chiefly by three rivers: the *Jordan, Weber,* and *Bear.* Other sources include springs, creeks, canals, direct rainfall, snowfall, and seepage.

The Great Salt Lake and Its Water Sources

Seasonal Variations in Depth

The condition of the shoreline, as well as the level of the lake, also changes with each season. Seasonally, the lake rises in the spring due to precipitation, and in the early summer due to snow-melt. The water level falls beginning in mid-summer and continues into winter. During a normal year a 3-4 foot fluctuation in lake elevation can occur.

The Great Salt Lake has no water outlet other than evaporation. The lake's level is dependent upon precipitation and evaporation rates.

A Unique Feature—Salt Crystal Polygons

Can we see numbers in nature? Yes, but they are not usually counted out for us. Mathematics in nature is often based upon a six-sided principle. Due to the process of upward capillarity and evaporation, mineral salts are deposited on the surface. Salt crystals grow

Salt crystal polygons lace the Salt Flats
west of the Great Salt Lake.

A close-up of a salt-crystal polygon network.

and build up pressure until the stress results in six-sided symmetrical formations, fitting adjacent hexagons perfectly. This effect is often evident on the Bonneville Salt Flats. The same six-sided (hexagonal) code is evident in honeycomb construction by bees.

Water that Doesn't Freeze

During the winter months, when the temperatures drop below freezing, the water of the Great Salt Lake does not freeze because of the water's high salinity. However, the temperature of the water is often below freezing, and may register in the 20s. This is why it is very dangerous to be on the lake during the cold winter months. A person who falls into the water in these extremely cold conditions can survive only a few minutes. When a person's body temperature is dramatically lowered due to the environment, the effect is called hypothermia.

*This photo shows ice on the surface
of the Great Salt Lake.*

Water that Does Freeze

But ice is sometimes seen on the Great Salt Lake. How does this happen?

Being lighter in weight than salt water, fresh water from rain, snow or tributaries will often collect and freeze on the lake's surface before having a chance to mix with the salt water. Also, ice formed on the incoming tributaries is often deposited onto the surface of the lake.

The Modern-day Flood Years

From 1982 through 1987, the Salt Lake area experienced a cool, wet cycle and the lake peaked 12 feet higher than its normal level (4,200 feet in elevation). Flooding around the lake was extensive. Since Great Salt Lake has a shallow basin, a 12-foot rise in water level covers an extensive amount of land.

*Ice on the water's surface has been heaped up
by wind and wave action and blown onto the shore.
Antelope Island and Frary Peak
are seen in the background.*

*Taken from I-80 looking east, this photo exhibits tell-tale
remnants of the Great Salt Lake flood.*

More than the size of the lake was affected during the flood years. The ecosystem was also thrown out of balance due to the increased amount of fresh water and decreased salinity. Thousands of acres of surrounding wildlife habitat were flooded.

Marshlands

Wetlands surrounding Great Salt Lake provide an excellent nesting environment for hundreds of thousands of birds, while the Great Salt Lake provides them food in the form of brine shrimp and brine flies. These marshy areas adjacent to the lake provide immense areas of wildlife habitat. The fresh water influence is backed by a very gradual decline toward the salty waters of Great Salt Lake. "Marshes are the single richest ecosystem yet defined in terms of available energy, even when compared with most types of intensive farming."[4]

The Fremont (early natives) built their villages and camps within the wetlands adjacent to the lake. These areas produced an abundance of food. "Site density in these marshes is as high or higher than any other region in Utah (including those occupied by the Anasazi) and it is almost impossible to distinguish one site from another along the length of the levees because they are so numerous," writes David Madsen, former state archaeologist (Stum, *Visions of Antelope Island*).

One of the most vital environmental concerns facing the wetlands surrounding Great Salt Lake and areas adjacent to the wetlands is the development (destruction) of agricultural lands by housing construction and the building of roads.

---

4. Odum, 1963. See Utah Geological and Mineral Survey, Bulletin 116, 1980.

Man's Early Influence on the Local Environment

At one time there were over 10,000 head of sheep on Antelope Island. Because of such overgrazing in a fragile environment, cheat grass, which is not a native species, has taken over. It is an annual grass species with only about a two to three week period when it is palatable. It goes to seed and dries up very early in the season, creating a large fire hazard. Many fires have occurred due to lightning strikes.

Cheatgrass is an undesirable plant, but it grows quickly and uses moisture more efficiently than perennial grasses, which hold more moisture in the soil. If it were not for this unusual annual grass species, however, the top soil would completely erode, leaving the land without the ability to support vegetation at all. The cheat grass at least stabilizes the top soil and keeps it in place.

Desert conditions are usually created by overgrazing. A desert is seldom a natural occurrence. Even the Sahara is man-made, caused mainly by the overgrazing of sheep. Due to harsh conditions, an arid region is very sensitive to any alteration. It is especially difficult for it to recover from damage like overgrazing. Once a region dries out, a self-destructive process results that grows like a cancer. Seeds can't germinate, and if they do, they cannot get established because the soil loses its ability to hold moisture.

Once vegetation is gone, the remaining roots dry out and become brittle, losing their ability to reinforce the soil. The soil hardens, which further inhibits new seeds from getting a foothold. Thus, when it rains—and it usually comes quick and hard in arid places—the weakened soil and remaining plant life are broken up and washed away. Exposed is an even harder ground, where seeds have less chance to germinate. The hardened and dry earth, without a "buffer"-type surface (topsoil and plantlife) cannot readily absorb water, so it cannot support plant life even if moisture is provided.

To demonstrate how desert soil is less capable of absorbing water, see Experiment 7 at the back of this book.

Water holes like this one are well-hidden within the Salt Lake desert due to the contour of the land and the bleak surroundings. There is no green vegetation except in close proximity to the water. This recessed pond is located near Knolls, Utah between Salt Lake City and Wendover.

7

Plant and Animal Life Around the Lake

Small and Microscopic Inhabitants

Brine shrimp, bacteria, protozoa, a blue-green algae, brine fly larvae, and a type of water beetle called corixid (which preys on brine shrimp and is more abundant when less saline conditions exist) are basically the only life forms in the Great Salt Lake. The lake's high salt content is too hostile for other forms of aquatic life.

The Rainwater Killi Fish

During the lake's rise in the years 1983 to 1987, the Great Salt Lake became diluted by freshwater enough to allow the Rainwater Killi fish to live in its waters for a short period. The Killi can tolerate a low percentage of salt content and lives in some of the brackish (stagnant, impure and somewhat salty) water surrounding Great Salt Lake. The Killi fish entered the Great Salt Lake from Timpie Springs in 1986 when the lake's salinity was at approximately 5.5 percent.

Animal Life

Muskrat, carp, and blackbirds (both yellow-headed and red-winged) are abundant in the drainage areas bordering the lake.

Great Salt Lake Bird Refuges

WMA = Waterfowl Management Area

The main concentration and greatest variety of wild-life exists on Antelope Island. The island has a population of about 700 buffalo, from which approximately 150 are sold each year. The herd compensates for this number sold by reproduction, increasing by about 150 annually.

Buffalo dusting themselves at the ranch on Antelope Island. A Russian Olive tree and the rock formation called Molly's Nipple are in the background.

About 60 pronghorn antelope exist on Antelope Island. California bighorn sheep were introduced in 1997. Their numbers have increased to about 80.

Mule deer number close to 200 and are commonly viewed on the island. These figures are for the year 2000 and will vary. Chukar Partridge are very abundant. Other wildlife in the lake region include squirrels, porcupine, coyotes, skunks, weasels, and mule deer.

Few foxes are seen on the island since coyotes (larger canines) keep them off. This, in turn, provides a better habitat for birds since foxes primarily feed on birds. Coyotes, in contrast, feed on many other animals.

Bird Life

The lake is surrounded by a great expanse of freshwater sloughs, canals, and other drainage systems which feed it. In these freshwater areas lie an abundance of aquatic wildlife. The irregular shoreline, with its extensive mud flats and marshes, along with a dozen islands that dot the lake, teem with bird life. At least 257 species of birds have been observed on the Great Salt Lake and in the surrounding freshwater marshy areas. Most use the lake as a stopping point during migrations. Many nest and stay most of the spring, summer, and fall, but very few species spend the winter.

Among the birds commonly seen are American avocets, eared grebes, terns, killdeer, snowy egrets, black-necked stilts, great blue herons, American white pelicans, Canadian geese, and many varieties of ducks. Upland game-birds are also plentiful in the bottom lands (farmlands) next to the marshes. Bird watching is a very popular activity around the edges of the Great Salt Lake.

Every year hunters are attracted to bird-refuge areas near the lake, where many upland game birds and all major species of waterfowl are found. Many ducks and geese are harvested each year during the October-to-December hunting season.

Migratory birds also use islands in the lake for spring and summer nesting, feeding on brine flies and brine shrimp. The birds are safe from predators on the islands. Several rookeries (extensive bird nesting areas) exist on the Great Salt Lake.

California gulls (the Utah State Bird) are abundant within the Great Salt Lake vicinity. They have been held in high regard ever since they destroyed a plague of crickets that threatened the crops of Mormon pioneers in 1848. California gulls can eat almost anything and don't have to leave the lake to feed. Herons, cormorants, terns, and pelicans, however, are fish-eaters. Pelicans, especially, work hard for enough to eat and feed their young, often traveling 80 to 100 miles to reach fresh-water areas for fish. They have a nine-foot wing span and migrate to Mexico during the winter months.

Several designated wetlands, bird refuges and water-fowl management areas surround Great Salt Lake.

A California gull hunts for food.

To get to the **Farmington Bay Bird Refuge** from north of Salt Lake City, use I-15; get off at exit 322; turn left (east) at the overpass; go to the Frontage Road traffic light and turn left (north) on Frontage road. Go past McDonalds until you get to Glovers Lane (several miles); turn left (west) at Glovers Lane, and travel along Glovers Lane until you get to 1325 West; then turn left (south) and travel through the gate. Hours are 8 a.m. to 5 p.m.

Algae and Bacteria

Twenty-nine species of algae have been identified in the Great Salt Lake. Bacteria live on the bottom of the lake where they produce calcium carbonate and build extensive rock-like accumulations (tufa) resembling the coral reefs of the ocean. Freshwater lake levels have produced most of these deposits, but smaller amounts are still being formed in the lake today. Algal bioherms, composed mainly of calcium and magnesium carbonates, are precipitated by living algae.

"Part of the dissolved salts, especially phosphate, nitrate, ammonium, and bicarbonate, is necessary for the growth of the algae and other organisms."[5]

The water of Great Salt Lake turns a deep green color in the spring and periodically during the summer and fall. This "pea soup" condition is created through the

The lighter masses are deposits of calcium carbonate (tufa) at the Bonneville level. (Danger Cave State Park, Wendover, Utah)

build-up of bacteria and algae. When the brine-shrimp eggs hatch and the brine-fly larva emerge, they feed on the algae. Great Salt Lake goes through several of these cycles during the warmer months of the year. The bacteria and algae are depleted by a mass reproduction of brine flies and brine shrimp. Then, because no food

---

5. Gwyn, J. Wallace, ed., (*Great Salt Lake*, a scientific historical and economic overview).

exists for these brine flies and brine shrimp, their numbers decrease to match the depleted food supply. When the bacteria and algae increase, the brine shrimp and brine flies also become more abundant. Spiders, predominantly the orb weaver, also benefit as a result of the brine flies that venture inland.

Brine Shrimp (*Artemia salina*)

The adult brine shrimp is about a half-inch long. Brine shrimp eggs are carried in a pouch in the rear of the mother's body. They are so small that about 150 could fit on the head of a pin. After hatching, they become adults in two to three weeks. They reproduce every two to three days, laying approximately 150 eggs at a time.

In the winter they die off, leaving their eggs to carry on their existence. These tiny, round eggs can remain dormant, but fertile, for many years, refusing to hatch unless conditions are just right (when water temperatures warm up in the spring). The ideal salinity level for them to hatch is about 16%. Eggs that do not hatch are often buried and become fossilized (calcified). This

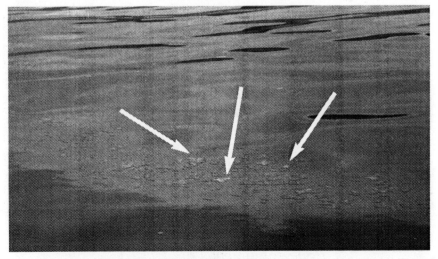

Brine shrimp eggs collect on the water's surface.

process contributes to the formation of oolitic sand, although most oolitic sand is formed from brine shrimp fecal pellets. The brine shrimp feed on microscopic bacteria and algae.

Brine shrimp are a major food supply for thousands of birds throughout the year, if not in the form of shrimp, in the form of eggs. Many birds, including ducks and gulls, are seen gathering brine shrimp and eggs in their bills. Because the water is so salty, some birds gather up the salt water with the eggs and separate the salt from their food by pressing their tongues against the roof of their mouths. In this way, they filter out most of the salty water surrounding the shrimp and their eggs.

The Brine Shrimp Industry

During the winter when the brine shrimp eggs become dormant and the brine shrimp die, the eggs are harvested, processed, dried, packaged and sold for fish food.

Brine-shrimp eggs are loaded
onto a truck from a boat.

They are shipped to the orient where they are hatched to feed prawns, crab and lobsters, or they are hatched and the tiny shrimp are processed into fish food (flakes) for home aquariums. From two to 12.5 million pounds of brine-shrimp eggs are harvested annually, producing an average income of $30 million.

The Brine Fly

The brine fly is a small fly (slightly smaller than the common housefly) indigenous to the Great Salt Lake. This insect is a major food source for many migratory birds within the inter-dependent ecosystem on the border areas of the lake.

Gulls are often seen half running and half flying along the lake shore with their mouths wide open, gathering brine flies as they swarm up from the water's edge. Brine flies help clean the lake by consuming lake wastes and algae. The brine flies remove more than 120,000 tons of organic material each year from Great Salt Lake. Organic wastes discharged into the lake are also assimilated by brine shrimp that consume bacteria and algae. Brine flies in turn provide food for amphibians, shore birds, waterfowl, mammals, reptiles, fish, spiders, and other insects as they fly to the adjacent shores and freshwater marshy areas.

Brine flies begin as tiny eggs in the salt water. They pass through a larva stage, feeding on algae and bacteria, then enter a floating pupa stage. After this, they hatch and swarm over the nearby shores by the millions. This process takes place within 36 hours.

Brine flies are not attracted to humans and prefer flying low to the ground. They do not bite, nor do they transmit disease. They are not attracted to human food. The adult flies live three to four days. By carrying their air supply in a bubble, brine-fly pupa feed on algae that exists below the water's surface. Their pupae cases are

Brine flies gather on the shore
of the Great Salt Lake.

attached to what are referred to as "reefs" on the lake bottom. When ready to emerge, creamy white adults make a hole in the case and pop out at the water's surface. As their new skin hardens, they turn a dark grey color. Storms wash pupae off the lake bottom and the wind blows them to shore. The Indians called them "Koo-Ts'abe" and gathered the pupae for food.[6]

The Smell of Decomposing Organic Material

An unpleasant odor sometimes emanates from the shores of the Great Salt Lake due to decaying plant and animal matter. This is only evident along the lake's shores, not in the lake or on the land. Once freshwater aquatic life reaches the salt water, it dies. Pupae cases, from which the brine fly hatch, and blue-green algae make up most of the organic material that accumulates

---

6. Robert N. Wingate, Brigham Young University.

*Blue-green algae decomposes
along the shores of the Great Salt Lake.*

*Decomposing brine fly pupae cases are abundant around
the shores of the Great Salt Lake.*

Blue-green algae, brine fly pupae cases, and dead fish (most likely carp coming into the lake from the surrounding brackish waters) are deposited along the shores.

and contributes to the decomposition zone. This material stagnates in pockets, sloughs, inlets, and other collection areas. An unpleasant odor results, especially during warm summer months when the decomposition process is the most active.

The Ecosystem Food Chain

Everything in nature plays an important role in the ecosystem and its food chain. Algae is consumed by brine shrimp and brine flies, which are, in turn, eaten by birds. Birds, their eggs and young are consumed by fox, weasels, skunks and other mammals. Many of the freshwater areas surrounding Great Salt Lake provide vegetation not found in the dry desert areas further inland. Deer, rabbits, squirrels, muskrat and other plant-eaters also exist in these areas.

Avocets search the shore for food.

Killdeer eggs, camouflaged as rocks, bask in the sun.
(Notice their size compared to the quarter.)

Three killdeer chicks—from the nest on the previous page—survive the dangerous lakeside environment.

Midge flies, mosquitoes, and gnats ("no-see-ums") are also common around the shores of Great Salt Lake, nourished by the freshwater marshy areas surrounding the lake.

What good are insects? Some consider them a pest and nuisance, but many species depend on them to live.

Many animals have adapted to a specialized diet. In the case of some birds, this may consist of certain insects or crustaceans. Through a biological and genetic process, over centuries of time, the animals become more efficient at procuring certain species as a main food source (diet). If this food source is threatened, whether it is an insect, fish, or small mammal, the special adaptation is a disadvantage. In the new ecological condition, the species is left with no way to cope. The special and specific adaptation of the species, which took thousands of years to perfect, is no longer useful, and the animal rejects the use of other food sources. Thus, if flies and brine shrimp were to be killed off, many Great Salt Lake shore birds could no longer exist.

Plant Life in the Transition Zone (Surrounding Edges of the Great Salt Lake)

Plants that tolerate a high percentage of salt are referred to as halophytes. Among these are pickleweed, salt grass, inkweed, greasewood, and iodine bush. Common freshwater marsh plants within the transition zone are cattail, bulrush, tamerisk, and fragmyties. The last two are plentiful, but not indigenous plants.

*Here, pickleweed grows amongst
brine fly pupae cases and salt crystals.*

Plant life inland includes sage brush, rabbit brush, and flowers such as globe mallow, blue flax, evening primrose, Indian paintbrush, and the western wall flower.

*Western
Wall Flower*

Indian Paintbrush

Evening Primrose

Part 3

Nature's Handiwork

Antelope Island

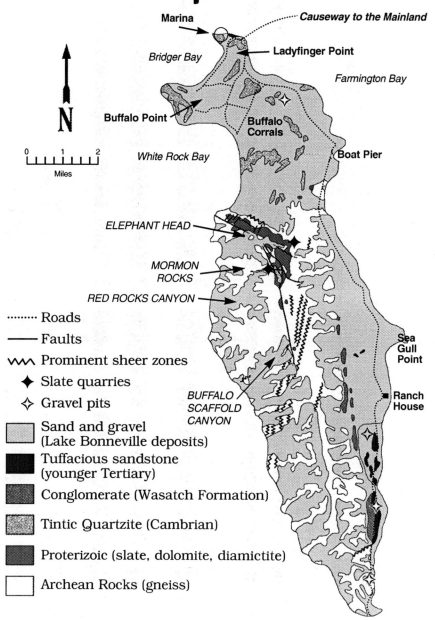

Marina

Causeway to the Mainland

Bridger Bay

Ladyfinger Point

Farmington Bay

N

Buffalo Point

Buffalo Corrals

0   1   2
Miles

White Rock Bay

Boat Pier

ELEPHANT HEAD

MORMON ROCKS

RED ROCKS CANYON

Sea Gull Point

········ Roads
———— Faults
〜〜 Prominent sheer zones
✦ Slate quarries
✧ Gravel pits

BUFFALO SCAFFOLD CANYON

Ranch House

▨ Sand and gravel (Lake Bonneville deposits)

■ Tuffacious sandstone (younger Tertiary)

▨ Conglomerate (Wasatch Formation)

▨ Tintic Quartzite (Cambrian)

▨ Proterizoic (slate, dolomite, diamictite)

□ Archean Rocks (gneiss)

8

Islands of the Great Salt Lake

Islands of the Great Salt Lake include *Antelope, Stansbury, Fremont, Carrington, Gunnison, Dolphin, Hat* (or Bird), *Badger, Egg, Cub, White Rock, Strong's Knob,* and *Black Rock.* They are listed in descending order, by size.

Antelope Island

Antelope Island is the largest island of Great Salt Lake. It is 16 miles long and a maximum of five miles wide. The island was given its name because it provided

The Great Salt Lake and Antelope Island.

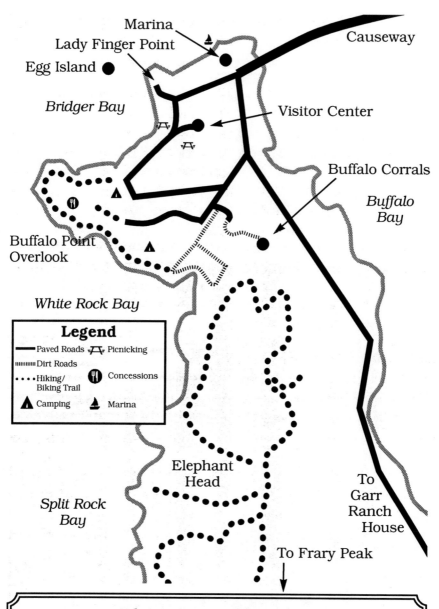

Close-up View of Recreational Sites on the North End of Antelope Island

John Fremont's surveying party antelope meat during a successful hunt. It consists of about 28,000 acres. It's highest elevation is 6,597 feet.

The whole island makes up the largest state park in Utah. The park has a marina located at its northern end.

Some of the oldest rocks in the world are found on Antelope Island. Referred to as the Farmington Canyon Complex, they are dated 2.8 to 3 billion years old. Beginning about mid-point on the island, they can be seen along the eastside road, just north of the Frary Peak turn-off.

The first human inhabitants of Antelope Island were hunters. Chief Wanship's son is the first "owner." Although native Americans did not understand the concept of owning land, he and his three wives had claim to

Fremont/Archaic Archaeological Collection, Antelope Island Visitor Center. All of the collection originates from Fremont Island. Courtesy of the Stoddard Family.

the island as their hunting grounds. After Fremont's successful hunt, Chief Wanship's son confronted Fremont demanding some kind of payment, which he received in the form of trading goods. Evidence so far suggests that Antelope Island was a hunting ground yearly visited, but without permanent occupancy.

Archeological digs in 1999 and 2000 reveal further evidence that Antelope Island served as a temporary hunting site for native people. In early 1999, in preparing to install the water system at Mushroom Springs for the Garr Ranch facility, an archeological site was discovered. The most valuable part of this discovery was the distinct stratification. The layers that mark the times the camp was occupied reveal recurring visits for hundreds of years. Items found at the site include deer

The Garr Ranch House
Notice the different additions and building construction
material. Starting from the left (south) is adobe brick made
in 1848, next is more adobe brick added on in 1880,
and the last addition is cinderblock in 1950.

bones, bowls, shards, arrow points, manos, metates and charcoal (evidence of fires).

The Garr Ranch, built in 1848 by Fielding Garr, operated under different names and ownership until 1981. Garr was commissioned as a licensed herdsman by Brigham Young to raise cattle to support the Perpetual Immigration Fund. This fund generated money by raising and selling livestock to finance Mormon immigration to Utah. Once they made the trip and became established, the immigrants would repay their debts to the fund. However, most ownership of the island was not by the Mormon church. In 1884 the John Dooly family acquired the island. In 1972 the Anachutz Family took over the island. Finally, in 1981, Antelope Island was purchased by the state of Utah for $4,700,000.

Stansbury Island

Named for Captain Howard Stansbury, this is the second largest island of Great Salt Lake. Although second in size, with 22,314 acres, Stansbury Island has the highest elevation: 6, 645 feet. The south-east side of the island is known for its petroglyphs. Part of the island is privately owned and the rest is managed by the BLM. Utah State parks and the BLM administer a biking trail that follows the Lake Bonneville terrace around the island.

Fremont Island

The third largest island of the Great Salt Lake, Fremont Island, is privately owned. The island consists of 2,945 acres. It's highest point is 4,995 feet.

A fair amount of history exists concerning the island. John Baptise, a grave robber who for several years stole from graves in the Salt Lake City cemetery, was exiled to Fremont Island in 1862. Judge Wenner and his family lived in a house on Fremont Island from 1886 to

1891. Wenner's grave is there, with his wife's ashes deposited beside him. Two natives, an 18-year-old adolescent and a 6-year-old child, are two other burials discovered on Fremont Island. The Stoddard Family leased Fremont Island from 1948 until 1960.

One of the state's most unique archaeological collections originated from Fremont Island. Earl Stoddard was the first to begin the collection. It is currently displayed as an exhibit in the Antelope Island visitor center. The collection was secured in 1999 by the author.

Carrington Island

Carrington Island is only 1,767 acres. Charles Stoddard built a cabin on the island in 1932 and lived there with his wife and three small children in an attempt to raise sheep. Due to a lack of water and predation by coyotes, his attempt failed. The island was used in the more recent past as a bombing range by the U.S. Air Force.

Gunnison Island

Gunnison Island is a small island consisting of 163 acres. Its highest point has an elevation of 4492 feet. This island was homesteaded in the 1890's by Alfred Lambourne for the purpose of planting a vineyard (1,000 grape vines). But when he discovered that not enough water was available to support their growth, the project was abandoned. Today, this island is a rookery for the American white pelican. By state regulation, public access is not allowed. It is closed off for a mile in every direction of the shoreline.

Dolphin Island

Dolphin Island consists of 60 acres and is 4,275 feet high. It received the name because it is shaped somewhat like a dolphin.

Bird Island

Bird (Hat) Island is 22 acres in size and is also 4,275 feet in elevation. Shaped like a hat, the island has served as a small nesting area for gulls and pelicans. By state regulation, public access is not allowed. It is also closed off for a mile in every direction of the shoreline.

Badger Island

Badger Island is 6 acres and 4,225 feet high. It was named after a person, not the animal.

Egg Island

This island is named for the 76 heron eggs taken by Stansbury's men during an early exploration. Barely an acre in size, depending on the lake's water level, Egg Island serves as a rookery for the California Gull and Great Blue Heron. The island is closed to public access from April through June for nesting.

Cub Island

Cub Island serves as another rookery, and is located just north of Gunnison Island in the north arm of the lake. By state regulation, public access is not allowed. It too is closed off for a mile in every direction of the shoreline.

White Rock

White Rock is basically a large rock in the midst of White Rock Bay located off the northwest shore of Antelope Island. It is white because it is coated with sea gull feces.

Strong's Knob and Black Rock

Strong's Knob and Black Rock have been considered islands, and qualify as such during high water levels. (Argument has it that if Stansbury Island consistently qualifies as an island, although much larger and with

Black Rock, looking north across Great Salt Lake.

much more area exposed to the lake, why wouldn't these qualify?)

It is not inaccurate to say that about a dozen islands exist within Great Salt Lake. Ten (eleven if we count Goose Island) are actually called islands. If the lake rises, some islands are created from peninsulas and others are covered. If the lake falls some islands emerge and others become peninsulas.

9
Weather

Tornadoes

It is not uncommon in the spring or fall, during unstable climatic weather, for tornadoes to form over the Great Salt Lake (referred to as water spouts when over the water). One such tornado, in 1999, damaged buildings, destroyed property, injured many people

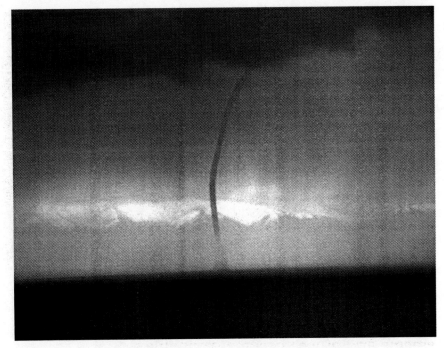

An eastbound tornado heads inland
from the Great Salt Lake. Viewed from Antelope Island.

and took the life of one individual when it moved east into downtown Salt Lake City.

Tooele Twister

A "Tooele Twister" is a strong, isolated storm that creates a "funnel" effect. It often originates in the area of Tooele when a larger weather system enters the area. A "Tooele Twister" can be very dangerous to boats on the Great Salt Lake.

Microbursts

A microburst is an isolated storm often caused by a single thunderhead cloud. It can produce strong winds, rain, and rough waters. Although usually of short duration (often only 15 to 20 minutes), the dangerous conditions caused by microbursts can capsize boats, run them aground, or drive them into other vessels.

An isolated storm moves east across the Great Salt Lake.

The "Lake Effect" on Local Weather

The lake often creates its own weather pattern. Wind is commonly caused by the difference in water and land temperatures. In the summer months, if no other weather influence exists, cool air from the lake flows inland during the day, then during the evening cool air from the mountains flows toward the lake.

The lake has a moderating effect on the extremely cold winter air. This influence affects the surrounding communities of the Wasatch Front. The lake's water temperature, although cold, is warmer than the winter

The "Lake Effect"

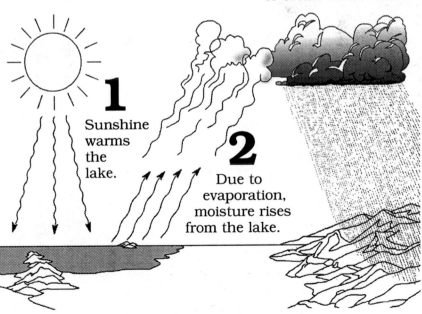

3

As moisture rises, it cools and condenses to create rain or snow.

1

Sunshine warms the lake.

2

Due to evaporation, moisture rises from the lake.

air. Evaporation (a steam effect) contributes to extremely heavy snowfalls.

During the winter, a big difference sometimes develops between the temperature of the lake water and the temperature of a passing overhead storm air mass. The warmer air directly over the lake rises into the colder stormy air causing a rapid updraft and subsequent heavier snow. When this "lake effect" occurs within a normally intense storm, the results can be extreme. More than 24 inches of snow often fall in a 24-hour period along the Wasatch mountain range. The same effect occurs along the shores of the eastern Great Lakes.

10

Other Physical Phenomena

Icebergs

The surface water temperature of the Great Salt Lake varies from the upper 20s (F) in January to about 75 to 80 degrees (F) in early August. When the water temperature is in the 20s, the lake does not freeze due

Charles Stoddard standing on a giant iceberg
that floated across the Great Salt Lake from the north
in 1942. According to Stoddard and Burt Paice,
it was 30 feet high and 100 feet square.

to the water's high salt content. However, icebergs reaching up to 30 feet high occasionally have been observed floating on the lake's surface. These are formed either from fresh water that collects from rain or snow; water that flows into the lake from tributaries, and freezes on the surface before mixing with the salt water; or from ice that has formed prior to entering Great Salt Lake. Wind and wave action can push the ice into mounds of incredible size.

Oolitic Sand

The sand particles of the Great Salt Lake form in the shallow offshore water. Each grain is called an oolite (egglike) and begins with a small nucleus or center particle on which outer layers of mineral deposits are collected. A brine shrimp fecal pellet is a common nucleus around which small crystals of calcium carbonate form within the lake's water. Calcified

This sand sculpture won First Place in the Beach Fest '95 non-castle sculpturing contest.

brine shrimp eggs also contribute to the sand medium. The constant shift of the sands within the lake serves to polish these grains of sand, resulting in perfectly formed, small round balls. Oolitic sand is excellent for sand sculpturing. This brings many people, locally and from out of state, to participate in sand sculpturing contests. Oolitic sand is also used to dry cut flowers.

Great Salt Lake's Buoyancy Effect

People float easily in the waters of the Great Salt Lake due to the lake's high salt content. It's actually very difficult for them to sink. One can literally "float like a cork"

A buoyancy experiment shows a boiled egg placed in a jar of fresh water (left), and another boiled egg placed in a 25 per cent salt-water solution (right).

in the waters of the Great Salt Lake. People come from all over the world to experience this effect.

However, the more diluted the salt water becomes with fresh water, the less buoyancy one has. Due to its higher percentage of salt content, the northern arm has a higher buoyancy factor than the southern arm.

The Lake's Colors

A large difference in salt content exists between the northern and southern arms of the lake. About 90 per cent of the lake's fresh water enters the southern half of the lake. This results in a constant flow of water northward through breaches in the causeway that separates the northern and southern arms. This causes a common difference of 10 per cent more salinity in the northern arm than in the southern arm.

The red coloration of the north arm of Great Salt Lake is a red algae and a halophyte bacteria that survive best in waters of 22% to 27% salinity. Blue-green algae can survive in the southern arm of the lake, but cannot live in the higher salt concentration of the northern half.

The Expansion Power of Crystallization

Earlier, we have seen how salt crystallization created a pressure which resulted in polygons on the surface of the Salt Flats. The pressure created by crystallization can be tremendous. Many of us have seen how water freezing in pipes can burst them. When water is caught in cracks of rocks, the expansion power that results from freezing can break the rock in half.

This same power exists in salt, as evidenced in fence posts within the Salt Flats. In the photo below, water rich in mineral salts was absorbed by the posts. When the wood dried, the salt crystallized. As it crystallized it expanded, splintering the wood.

Salt Flats along I-80 looking east.
Fence posts are blasted apart by salt crystallization.

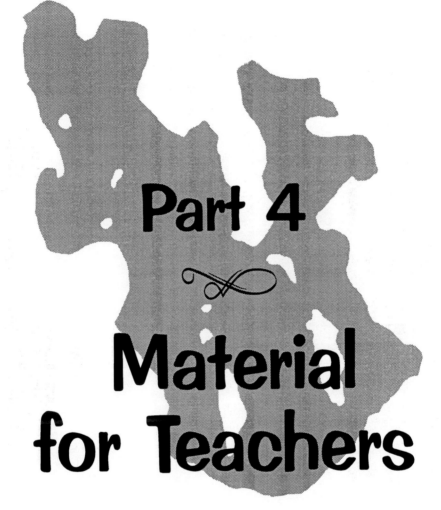

Part 4

Material for Teachers

11

Educational Resources, Self-guided Tours and Field Trip Opportunities

Recreation and Boating

To get to **Antelope Island State Park and Marina,** leave I-15 at exit number 335, turn west and continue on Antelope Drive until reaching the park entrance. ($7.00 day-use entrance fee, 2000.) After traveling seven miles across the Davis County causeway, take the right fork of the road another mile to the visitor center.

To get to the **Great Salt Lake State Marina,** take I-80 west from Salt Lake City to exit 104, Saltair Drive (SR 202), approximately 16 miles. Turn right at the off-ramp stop sign, then take a left at the second stop sign and follow the roadway west to the marina.

Saltair, the only remnant of the historical lake resorts, is also located off Interstate 80, about 16 miles west of Salt Lake City, at exit 104. Take a right at the end of the freeway off-ramp, then, after the stop sign, continue straight into Saltair's parking lot. Salty's Gifts is located outside (south) of the Saltair pavilion in the paddle wheel boat. Within the Saltair pavilion is anoth-

er giftshop and snackbar. The pavilion sometimes hosts dances and concerts.

Willard Bay's **North Marina** is 15 miles north of Ogden, just off Interstate 15. The South Marina is eight miles north of Ogden.

Salt Island Adventures is a cruiseliner and tour service that operates out of the Great Salt Lake Marina. Features include murder mystery cruises,

Captain Steve Ingram pilots his boat,
The **Island Serenade,** *into the sunset for a dinner cruise.*

dinner, fireworks (July 4th and 24th), cruises for holidays, the full moon, hunters' widows, a "Santa Cruise," and a "Magical Cruise."

The boat can be chartered privately for weddings, company parties, birthdays, or any special occasion. For information and reservations, call (801) 252-9336, or make an internet visit at www.gslcruises.com.

Refuges and Nature

The *Ogden Nature Center* is located at 966 West 12th Street, and is easily accessible from I-15 via the 12th Street exit. The facility is open to the public Monday through Saturday, 10:00 a.m. to 4:00 p.m.

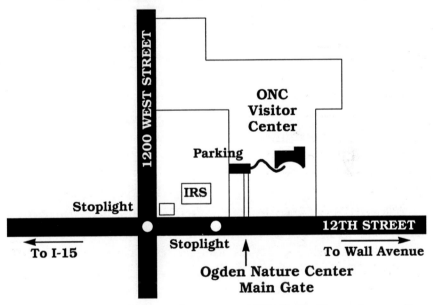

The *Bear River Migratory Bird Refuge* lines the eastern edge of the Promontory Mountains. Federal Highway 91, westbound from Brigham City, will get you there. See map on page 62.

The *Farmington Bay Waterfowl Management Area* lies at the south-east end of Farmington Bay, on the outskirts of Farmington, at exit 326 from I-15.

The **Ogden Bay Waterfowl Management Area** is west of Ogden, Roy and Plain City.

The **Locomotive Springs Waterfowl Management Area:** I-84 exits 7 or 16 will lead you to back roads that will take you 15 or 20 miles south-west to this refuge.

Layton Wetlands Preserve (The Nature Conservancy): Layton is about six miles north of Farmington. Educational tours can be arranged by appointment.

Railroad History

The **Golden Spike National Historic Site** is the predecessor to the railroad trestle and causeway.

Going south on I-84 from Tremonton, take local highway 83 at Blue Creek (exit 24), and head south past Howell. After about 15 miles, take a right to Promontory. Golden Spike is about five miles beyond that.

Going north on I-15, take local highway 83 at exit 368 and head east through Corinne. The turn-off to Promontory is about 20 miles from the freeway.

The **Ogden Union Station,** located at 2501 Wall Avenue, has two giftshops, a restaurant, a rocks and gems exhibit room, a railroad museum, and the **Browning Arms Museum** on the main floor. Ph. 393-9882

The Salt Lake City **Rio Grande** building, located at 270 South Rio Grande (500 West), offers a restaurant, museum, giftshop and exhibits on the first floor. The State Historical Society is located on the second floor, Ph. 533-3500 and 364-3302 (Cafe).

The **Tooele Railroad Museum** is located in downtown Tooele on Broadway and Vine streets. The facility is open Tuesdays through Saturdays, 10am to 4pm, Memorial Day through Labor Day. Call 882-2836 for more information.

Lakeside Factories

The **Kennecott/Bingham Copper Mine**—the world's largest open-pit copper mine—is located on the east slopes of the Oquirrh Mountains, west of Salt Lake City. It can be accessed from State Highway 48, or the New Bingham Highway, which can be found off I-15 at exit 301. Contact Kennecott for literature and touring information.

Morton Salt is located adjacent to I-80 on the north side of the freeway. Take exit 84, #138, west Grantsville exit off of I-80.

The **Benson Grist Mill** is located north of Grantsville on SR 138. Open Tuesdays through Saturdays, 10 am to 4pm, Memorial Day through Labor Day. Call 882-7678 for scheduling tours and more information.

Museums and Gift Shops

The **Hill Air Force Museum** is located in Roy, just east of Antelope island. Contact Hill Air Force Base for more information.

The **Donner-Reed Museum** is located in downtown Grantsville on the corner of Cooley and Clark streets. Call Ruth Matthews for tours at 884-3348.

The **Syracuse giftshop/bed and breakfast** is located on the north side of main street (Antelope Drive) in Syracuse. Phone 775-9114.

The **Children's Museum of Utah** is located at 840 north, 300 west (This street turns into Beck Street further north). Take the 6th north exit off I-15 east to Highway 89 and turn North. Follow the signs. Phone 322-5268 (information) and 328-3383 (office).

The **Museum of Natural History** is located at the University of Utah, President's Circle. Ph. 581-4303.

The **Hansen Planetarium** is located at 15 south State Street, Salt Lake City. Ph. 538-2104.

The **Layton Heritage Museum** is located at 403 Wasatch Drive at the city park just northwest of the high school. Call 546-8579.

Miscellaneous Information and Activities

The **Salt Lake Conventions and Visitors Bureau** has a visitor information center located off of Interstate 80 at 7200 west. Ph. 521-6110. Their main office is located at 90 South West Temple, Salt Lake City. Ph. 534-4903.

12

Study Questions on the Great Salt Lake

1. What causes the Great Salt Lake to be so salty?

2. In what zone (water, beach, land, or areas in between) does the major concentration of life exist in the Great Salt Lake ecosystem?

3. What causes the strong odor around Great Salt Lake?

4. What is the "lake effect"?

5. Where does the water come from that feeds Great Salt Lake?

6. How big is Great Salt Lake?

7. How big was Lake Bonneville?

8. How deep is Great Salt Lake?

9. How deep was Lake Bonneville?

10. What role does Great Salt Lake play in supporting wildlife?

11. What man-made barrier divides Great Salt Lake into its northern and southern arms?

12. Which of the arms has the highest salt content? Why?

13. If the Great Salt Lake water doesn't freeze due to its high salt content, why is there sometimes ice on the lake during the winter?

14. How many lakes still remain that are remnants of Lake Bonneville? Name them.

15. What is the highest salt content water can hold? Why?

16. How many species of birds rely on Great Salt Lake as part of their yearly life cycle?

17. What type of large mammals coexisted with humans 12,000 years ago? How were these animals hunted?

18. What bird calls Great Salt Lake its home and is Utah's state bird?

19. What major factor causes the difference in color between the northern and the southern arms of Great Salt Lake?

20. What type of native American culture first existed in the Great Salt Lake area?

21. What type of climate existed during the Lake Bonneville era?

22. What type of fish, from which fossils have been found, existed in Lake Bonneville?

23. How many state park facilities exist on Great Salt Lake?

24. What area makes up Antelope Island State Park?

25. Where is the Great Salt Lake Marina?

26. What is oolitic sand? How is it formed?

27. For what activity is oolitic sand popular?

28. Why is Great Salt Lake referred to as America's inland sea? List all the similarities to other seas that you can think of.

29. What is a "Tooele Twister"?

30. Why is it important to have radio communications while boating on Great Salt Lake?

31. Which channel is used for emergency communications?

32. How many state marinas exist on Great Salt Lake?

33. What kinds of mammals live around Great Salt Lake, including Antelope Island?

34. Name at least four birds that are commonly found on the shores of Great Salt Lake and in the fresh-water marshy areas bordering Great Salt Lake.

35. Why does the water of Great Salt Lake turn a deep green color in the spring?

36. If all the brine shrimp die during the winter, how is it possible that they reappear the next year?

37. What life exists in the water of Great Salt Lake? Can this ever change?

38. What is a rookery?

39. Give an example of a rookery on Great Salt Lake.

40. Define these terms:
   Brackish, Salinity, Nucleus, Hypothermia, Halophyte, Microburst.

Answers

1. A small amount of mineral salt is present in the freshwater which flows into the Great Salt Lake. Evaporation is the only outlet for the lake's water; when the water evaporates, the salt is left behind.

2. The heaviest concentration of life exists in the marshy areas surrounding the lake, between the shores of the lake and freshwater tributaries. This is the transition zone bordering the Great Salt Lake where freshwater marshy areas are backed up before entering the lake.

3. The smell is created by decaying plant and animal material. Once freshwater aquatic life reaches the salt water, it dies. Brine fly pupa cases and blue-green algae collect in piles along the shores of Great Salt Lake, which sources contribute the most to the decomposing organic material and its associated odor.

4. The term "lake effect" refers to the effect Great Salt Lake has on local weather. Caused by a difference in water temperature (warmer) and atmospheric temperature (cooler), it results in heavier snowfall along the Wasatch Mountains.

5. The water that feeds Great Salt Lake comes primarily from three major tributaries: the *Jordan, Weber,* and *Bear* rivers. Water also enters the lake from seepage, springs, creeks, and canals, and directly from rain and snow.

6. Great Salt Lake is approximately 90 miles long from north to south, and 40 miles wide from east to west. The area varies, depending on the lake's elevation.

7. Lake Bonneville covered about 20,000 square miles of land, an area that now consists of parts of Idaho, Nevada, and almost half of Utah.

8. When the lake's level is at 4,200 feet, the deepest part of the lake is about 34 feet.

9. Judging by the present lake level and the elevation of Lake Bonneville, and without taking into account sedimentation, the deepest point of Lake Bonneville was approximately 1,000 feet.

10. The lake is the sole source of brine flies and brine shrimp, which feed millions of birds and other primary creatures, supporting a complex ecosystem. The lake also supports an immense wildlife habitat around its edges.

11. The Lucin Cut-off, which is a causeway built by the Southern Pacific Railroad.

12. Northern. Approximately 90% of the lake's water enters the southern arm of the lake, causing the level in this part to rise faster. A continued drainage through the breaches in the railroad causeway carries much of the salt northward, and deposits it into the northern arm.

13. Fresh water either accumulates on the lake's surface and freezes before mixing with the salt water, or freezes prior to entering the lake in the form of snow, or ice is deposited by tributaries.

14. Three. Great Salt Lake, Utah Lake, and Sevier Lake.

15. 27.3 per cent. Once the salt content reaches that point it crystallizes and becomes a solid. This is also referred to as the saturation point.

16. 257 species.

17. Large mammals included the Monroe bear, ancient camel, woolly mammoth, a small horse, and

musk ox. As big game hunters, ancient people used fluted spear points.

18. The California Gull.

19. The amount of salt contained in the water. The northern arm has a salt content approximately 10 per cent higher than the southern portion. The salinity of the southern arm permits the existence of blue-green algae. The salinity level in the northern arm is too high for blue-green algae, but not for reddish-colored bacteria and algae. This explains the common red tones of the northern arm, and the blue-green color of the southern half.

20. Nomadic, Paleo-Indian/big game hunters. Their modern-day descendants are believed to be the Goshutes, Paiutes, Shoshonis, and Utes.

21. A somewhat humid climate.

22. The Bonneville cutthroat trout.

23. Two. *Great Salt Lake State Marina* and *Antelope Island State Park.* Although *Willard Bay State Park* borders the lake to the northeast, Willard Bay Reservoir is a freshwater body allowing no access to Great Salt Lake.

24. All of Antelope Island.

25. Great Salt Lake Marina borders I-80 approximately 17 miles west of Salt Lake City, along the south shore of Great Salt Lake.

26. Oolitic sand is formed in the Great Salt Lake. Mineral salts (crystals of calcium carbonate) gather around a nucleus, usually a brine shrimp fecal pellet. Some of the sand is likely old (calcified) brine shrimp eggs. The sand is polished and refined by the wave action of the Great Salt Lake.

27. Oolitic sand is popular for sand sculpturing, having the right texture and consistency to attract

professional sand sculptors from out of state to compete for prizes in sand-sculpting contests. It is also used to dry cut flowers.

28. It has many of the same characteristics as a sea: its size, the fact that it has its own water currents and wind patterns, it influences weather, it is salty, and has waves known to reach 18 feet high during severe storms. A type of shrimp also lives in Great Salt Lake, another similarity to the ocean.

29. A "Tooele Twister" is a strong, isolated storm, with a "funnel effect," which originates near Tooele when a larger weather system enters the area.

30. Sudden storms can develop on the lake, leading to the need to contact emergency rescue personnel and call for help.

31. U.S. Coast Guard Channel 16.

32. Two, one at *Great Salt Lake Marina* and one at *Antelope Island State Park.*

33. Fox, muskrat, weasel, squirrels, porcupine, skunks. Antelope Island has mule deer, buffalo, pronghorn antelope, rabbits, bighorn sheep, bobcat and coyotes.

34. Yellow-headed blackbirds, great blue herons, red-winged blackbirds, snowy egrets, black-necked stilts, Canada geese, American white pelicans, American avocets, California gulls, and many varieties of ducks.

35. Because of the build-up of bacteria and algae. When the brine shrimp eggs hatch and the brine fly larva emerge, they feed on the algae and the water clears up. This cycle occurs several times during the warmer months of the year.

36. Although the brine shrimp die off every year, eggs laid during the late summer go dormant over winter. When the saltwater reaches the right temperature in the spring, the eggs begin to hatch.

37. Basically, a blue-green algae, brine shrimp, and brine fly larva.

Yes, it can change. During the rise of lake water from 1984 to 1987, the Great Salt Lake became diluted by freshwater enough to allow the Rainwater Killi fish into its waters. The Killi is a fish that can tolerate a low percentage of salt content and still lives in some of the brackish waters surrounding Great Salt Lake.

38. A rookery is an area containing many bird nesting sites.

39. Egg Island.

40.   *Brackish:* Stagnant, impure, and somewhat salty water.

Salinity: Percentage of salt content.

Nucleus: A center particle, as in oolitic sand, around which mineral deposits accumulate.

Hypothermia: A condition in which one's body core temperature falls to a life-threatening level, affecting one's behavior, mental state, and physical condition.

Halophyte: A plant capable of thriving in salt-infested soil or water (e.g., the algae in the northern arm).

Microburst: An isolated storm, often caused by a single thunderhead cloud, producing strong winds, rain, and rough waters.

13

Experiments and Displays Relating to the Great Salt Lake

Experiment 1
The Evaporation Effect

To show the evaporation effect of a large, shallow lake compared to a deep lake, take a jar and a plate, placing equal amounts of water in both of them. Compare the two, and mark their levels. Notice the difference of evaporation after three days. Like the effect that takes place with Great Salt Lake, the water surface area of the plate is much greater than that of the jar, thus exposing more water to the air and creating a higher water temperature, which greatly contributes to evaporation.

Experiment 2
The Nucleus of Sand Particles

To see the original nucleus around which an individual oolitic grain of sand was formed, place several grains of sand in a small bowl of vinegar. Within a day, the nucleus should be revealed.

Experiment 3
The Buoyancy Effect

To demonstrate the increased buoyancy of highly concentrated salt water compared to freshwater, place a boiled egg in a clear jar filled with freshwater, then place another boiled egg in a jar filled with salt water (about a 1/5 salt to 4/5 water concentration ratio). Notice how the first egg sinks in fresh water and how the other egg floats in the salt water.

Experiment 4
Extracting Salt from Water

To show how salt is taken from the waters of the Great Salt Lake, fill a clear bowl half full of salty water (1/5 salt to 4/5 fresh water). Allow it to sit on a classroom table or countertop for several days (duration depends on room temperature and humidity). Watch as the solution evaporates and the salt crystals begin to appear. If a string is suspended in the water, salt crystals will form on it.

Experiment 5
Creating Lake Levels (Bench Marks)

Fill a tub or 6"-deep basin half full of water, and fill one end to the top with sand. Allow the sand to settle, then form wave action by using a fan or by simply using the palm of your hand to cause some rough water. After a "bench" is formed, extract enough of the water to allow the level to drop an inch or two, and try some more wave action. This process can be repeated, depending on the depth of the basin used.

Experiment 6
Evaporation

Fill three shallow pans with a half inch of water. Place one in the refrigerator and the other two outside in warm sunshine. Place a fan over one of these; the other should be protected from any wind. One day later, compare the three pans.

The water in the refrigerator did not evaporate much, because of the cool air. The water in the sun evaporated more because of the warmth. But the fan, combining heat, dry air and a higher volume of air mass to the water surface, accelerated the evaporation process in the third pan.

Experiment 7
Water Absorption

To show how dried, desert soil can lack the ability to absorb water, pour one cup of water onto a completely dry sponge and one cup onto a damp sponge. Compare the receptive qualities of each. The dry, harder sponge will expel the water, while the moist sponge will more readily absorb the water.

Bibliography

Brinkley, Alan, *The Unfinished Nation—A Concise History of the American People*. New York: Columbia University, McGraw-Hill Inc., 1993.

DeLafosse, Peter H., Editor, *Trailing the Pioneers*. Logan: Utah State University Press, and Utah Crossroads, Oregon-California Trails Association,1994.

Egan, Ferol, *Fremont, Explorer for a Restless Nation*. Reno: University of Nevada Press, 1977.

Gwyn, Ph.D., Wallace J., *Great Salt Lake—a Scientific, Historical and Economic Overview*. Salt Lake City: Department of Natural Resources, Utah Geological and Mineral Survey Bulletin 116, 1980.

Hassibe, W.R. and Keck, W.G., *The Great Salt Lake*. Denver: U.S. Geological Survey, Revised Printing, 1991.

Holt, Clayton, *History of Antelope Island (1840-1995)*. Syracuse: The Syracuse Historical Commission, Third edition, 1996.

Maxwell, James A., Editor. *America's Fascinating Indian Heritage—The First Americans: Their Customs, Art, History and How They Lived*. Pleasantville: Reader's Digest Association, 1978.

Miller, David E., *Great Salt Lake—Past and Present*. Sixth edition. Salt Lake City: Publishers Press, 1997.

Nevins, Allan, *Fremont, Pathmaker of the West*. Lincoln: University of Nebraska, 1955.

Stewart, George R., *Ordeal By Hunger*. Boston: Pocket Books, 1936.

Stokes, William Lee, *The Great Salt Lake*. Salt Lake City: Starstone Publishing Co., 1984.

Stum, Marlin, *Visions of Antelope Island and Great Salt Lake.* Logan: Utah State University Press, 1999.

The Great Salt Lake, America's Dead Sea (video). Ogden: Concepts Wisdom Enterprises, 1988.

Wharton, Tom, "Utah's Amazing Inland Sea." Salt Lake City: *Salt Lake Tribune,* Special Edition, 1992.

Williams, Terry Tempest, *The Desert Sea Seminar.* Salt Lake City: University of Utah, Fall, 1993.

Consulting Authorities

Birdsey, Paul, Educator
Department of Natural Resources
Division of Wildlife Resources

Brimhall, Rosie
Salt Lake Conventions and Visitors' Bureau

Bureau of Land Management

Casjens, Laura
Utah Museum of Natural History

Currey, Don
Geography Department, University of Utah

Department of the Interior

Donner/Reed Museum, The.
Grantsville, Utah

Geology and Antelope Island State Park
Davis County, Utah

Hill, Greg
Department of the Interior
Bureau of Land Management
Salt Lake City Office, Utah

Mathews, Ruth
The Donner/Reed Museum, Grantsville, Utah

Nature Conservancy, The

Paul, Don, Biologist
Department of Natural Resources
Division of Wildlife Resources

Salt Lake Tribune

Thompson, Bruce, Educator,
Friends of Great Salt Lake
P.O. Box 2655
Salt Lake City, Utah 84110

U.S. Geological Survey

Utah Department of Natural Resources

Utah Division of Parks and Recreation
Utah Division of Wildlife Resources
Utah Geological and Mineral Survey
Utah Museum of Natural History
Utah Wetlands Foundation
Wingate, Robert N.
   Brigham Young University, Provo, Utah

Index

About the Author

Alan Millard has worked for several natural resource agencies. He began with the National Park Service as a back-country ranger in Colorado, then worked as a Washington State Park Ranger. After this he worked for the Bureau of Land Management in Nevada, and as a park ranger in Utah. He has had many years of experience in public relations and education. Mr. Millard also teaches college.

He holds a Bachelor's degree in Natural

*The author
and his daughter, Melinda*

Resources from Western Washington University, has completed graduate courses in anthropology from the University of Utah, and holds a Master's degree in Organizational Management from the University of Phoenix.

Mr. Millard has been active in various projects designed to preserve the history and environment. He served as a committee team member in an effort to preserve the historical, cultural and natural resource values of the Wendover area, including interests such as the

Enola Gay Hanger, Danger Cave and Juke Box Cave, the Bonneville Salt Flats, the Donner-Reed immigrant party's Hastings Cut-off trail, the Pilot Peak landmark and the Bonneville Speedway. He also developed a self-perpetuating miniature environment of the Great Salt Lake and has secured the Fremont Island archaeological exhibit, for which project he helped prepare and write the text. These exhibits are featured at the Antelope Island Visitor Center and are frequently visited by university students and professors as well as the general public.

Mr. Millard has had many articles published and has been a guest speaker on several radio talk shows. He has done news announcements concerning local events and has appeared on television for environmental news shorts. He also has conducted many presentations pertaining to both political issues and natural resource education. He is the author of the book, *Equality: A Man's Claim,* which addresses the equality issue from the male perspective.